My Poem Book

Akshara Yogesh Kolekar

Society for Legal Education, Training & Research, Satara

My Poem Book

Akshara Yogesh Kolekar

Society for Legal Education, Training & Research, Satara

Society for Legal Education, Training & Research, Satara

Copyright © Akshara Yogesh Kolekar

Editorial Board

<u>Chief Editor</u>

Savita Yashvant Kale

Founder Member
Society For Legal Education, Training & Research

<u>Student Editorial Board</u>

Shardul Shashank Jangam

Sarthak Sudhir Tarlekar

Harshwardhan Rajesh Todkar

Aksh Subhash Miniyar

Jayvardhan Rajesh Todkar

Shreyaa Laxman Pawar

Aayush Anil Karve

<u>Preface</u>

Writing is one of my hobbies and I have been writing small poems since I was 6 years old.

Before this summer vacation, our Respected Principal Megha Pawar Madam of our School and my school teachers have suggested us to utilize our time in a fruitful manner so I was searching for a tool to use my summer holiday time in a best possible way. My parents suggested me to make good use of my hobby, thus started my writing journey. My dad and mom supported my idea and cheered me.

I am thankful to Dr Sujata Pawar Madam for motivation and encouragement. I am also very thankful to my teachers for teaching us the importance of time.

I am also thankful to the members of the editorial board who have contributed in the completion of the book.

My special thanks to my lovingly mom, the chief editor of the book, who has always stood by me and motivated me to complete the book. Thank you.

Akshara Yogesh Kolekar

<u>Oh Moon</u>

Oh moon oh oh moon

Show the way to the traveler in the
sparkly night

Shine bright together with your
teammates

The stars

Oh moon oh oh moon

The only hope of us in the night

Oh moon you're the prettiest thing
I have ever saw

Come to me

Take me to a ride across the world

Where sun is shining bright

Oh moon oh oh moon

Make sleep the little ones

Don't hide behind those clouds

Oh moon oh oh moon

****

Best Friend

Something rare, very special,

A really fortunate one gets

A best friend like mine, who cares
for you,

Sits with you, no matter what is
always on your side

My best friend sits with me shares
everything with me

Most importantly in friendship

Never envies me

Oh I am very lucky

That I got a good bestie

Something special, very rare, a really fortunate one get. I am the fortunate one

****

Mother

The one who loves us even when we are naughty,

An angel god has sent as a gift for me

A mother

Who is powerful than everyone

I love my mom very much

Sometimes she scolds us but

For our own good, sleeping without

their mother for children is a

nightmare

She will protect us no matter what.

Oh oh oh I love my mom very much.

****

<u>Tip Top Rain</u>

Tip top tip top

Magical water drops falling from
heaven

Pouring itself on our umbrellas, all
over the towns

Tip top tip top

Getting wet in the rain

Peter patter peter patter rain
falling on our heads

Tip top tip top

Magical water drops falling from heaven

Making us pure as it is

Making us fresh with hope

Tip top tip top

Magical water drops falling from heaven

Importance of Time

Tick tok tick tok

Clock goes on and on

Second by second, minute by minute,
hour by hour

Pendulum strikes at 12o' clock

The time is not stopping

My life is just going on and on

Now I know the importance of the time in my life

Tick tok tick tok clock goes on and on

****

The Autobiography of Fire

I am the fire

Which turns night into day

Now you must be wondering how a
night turns into a day

According to scientist

Sun is a burning ball which burns
burns and burns

I am the fire

Which makes heaven and hell

Which makes gods and devils

Which is a sign of power

I am the fire

I am the fire a important part ritual

I am considered as sacred, holly and
pure

I am the fire which is considered as
glory

A sign of victory

I am the fire

I am the fire which destroyed the
ravanas lanka

I am the fire which gives you heat
and light

I am the fire which makes you happy

When you celebrate bonfire with
your near ones

I am the fire which can destroy the
world

If gone uncontrolled

So respect me, get blessed by me

But don't play with me

Because I am the fire

I am made by the nature

I am the fire

****

<u>Wonderful Nature</u>

Oh wonderful nature oh wonderful nature

Thank you for proving food, water, medicines

And most important for survival

The oxygen

Oh wonderful nature oh wonderful nature

Thanks for giving us plants and trees which bear beautiful flowers juicy fruits and nutritious veggies

Oh wonderful nature oh wonderful nature

Thanks for giving us beautiful sceneries all around the world

Some can go on vacations here

Some can draw paintings here

Some can relax here

Oh wonderful nature oh wonderful nature

Thanks for giving us this birds whose sweet chirping makes us feel wonderful

Oh wonderful nature oh wonderful nature

My dearest thanks to you for everything

Oh wonderful nature oh wonderful nature oh wonderful nature

****

<u>The Mystery....?</u>

Lately I have been wondering about
my life

The harder I try it remains a
mystery

Oh what are you mystery

Always worrying me about my
grades

Just open up to us

Oh what are you mystery?

Am I selected or not?

Did I won the medal or not?

The harder I try it remains a
mystery

Oh what are you mystery?

I have been always thinking about
you mystery

Life is a mystery

Without it, it will not be a secrecy

****

<u>History</u>

The older I get the boring this
subject becomes

I don't understand its use

Teachers says it's really important

So I opened the book

A word didn't got into my head

I wish if it spoke itself

Hisstoryyyyy what is your mystery

Please introduce yourself

I always get sleepy when I touch
the textbook

Oh yeah I am not giving up on you
easily

So I tried to learn you

But your years and spelling were so
hard to remember and pronounce it

Because of you I remember my
ancestry

Daddy given a tip to become history
for myself

You became fun
And easy to learn

On the day of results I got a 00

And just one in front of it

I got 100%

Since that day

Oh hisstoryyyyy you became my
favorite subject

Hisstoryyyyyyyyy what are you
really?

Because you were always a mystery

****

<u>Surprises</u>

My dad given me a surprise

It was a beautiful blue shiny bicycle

My mom told me to wait for
Christmas for another present

But on my birthday

I got a surprise granny was visiting
and said she will bring me something

I kept wondering that what this
surprise will be

After a lot of thought I understand

that surprises are a mystery

Which is hard to solve

But in the end granny gave me a new

dress

Surprises are the biggest mystery

They make us happy

This mystery has been unfold....,

That is whatever the gift suprises

makes us happy

****

<u>Mr. Sparkles</u>

There was cat in our society whose
fur was really sparkly

Everyone from children to elderly
knew Mr. Sparkles

This cat was having a attitude

Which was extraordinary

If someone called him just sparkles
he used to ignoreee them

Unless they call him Mr. sparkles

This cat was so lovely to the ones
who used to call him King Mr.
Sparkles

I know

This cat had a bad attitude

But his fur was so shiny no one
stayed mad at him

There was cat in our society whose
fur was really sparkly

He was known as Mr. Sparkles

Oh My Daddy

Oh my hero

The one I feel safe with

A companion and a guide

The most wonderful friend and also
a mentor

The biggest motivation in my life

The best person I have ever met

The one I can trust

Oh my hero

oh my daddy

Sometimes you scold me

but I don't take it to my heart

Because I know you scold me for my
own good

oh my lovely daddy

oh my hero

****

<u>Story of Smart Printer</u>

Since childhood in terms of writing

I wanted to be like a printer

Because I thought there is a little

fairy like Tinkerbelle who lives

inside

Whose superpower is to write

swiftly

Whenever I give a command

whether colorful or black and white

it would give me the same hard copy

Also not only one fairy lived inside

other was good at drawing

she used to draw pictures of
whatever I wished

It was like I was the queen

but when I became a little older

I understand that no fairies lived
inside

The real reason is that the printer
has a high iq

The printer is very smart

But I am its Queen

This is the story of smart printer

****

<u>Exams......</u>

It's on its way

It's on its way

Exams omg exams

Teacher saying do study and
revisions

The exams gonna be offline

Me and my friends wondering about
online exams

How they were easy

Because of the MCQ type

Now all day and all night

We have to study and study

For the descriptive type

It's on its way

Like a parcel we ordered

Exams oh exams

I hope you are easy this time

But fun fact you are never easy
than before

Just getting harder and harder
each year

Showing us that we are growing up

Missing the abcd ... the alphabets

Studying for easiest subject first

Marathi, hindi , English, Ict then
geography ,civics and history and
then my favourite science and at
last in which I get tired mathssssss

Exams omg exams

It's on its way

****

My Surprise Smart Phone

A gift for my birthday

A smart phone

Mamma papa said that I will a get phone

I was just 5 then

I wondered what brand it will be

What color it will be

My mom asked which color I wanted

I was so happy

On my birthday I got my gift

Yes it was a smart phone of pink
color

Only one thing was different

Its brand was a toy brand

What did you thought?

That I will get a real phone

but

It was a toy phone

A gift for my birthday

A surprise

Oh yes

****

The Sports

Bored by sitting every day?

Let's go and play something

Wondering what to play

Oh don't worry we have many games

and sports to play

Such as badminton, tennis,

swimming, basketball and everyone's

favorite cricket

Wondering with whom to play

Oh don't worry we have got our colony pals, who always loves to play with us

Wondering playing individual or team sport

Oh don't worry you can play both

But these games are not sport

Sports are the one you play professionally.

Such as Saina Nehwal , Sachin Tendulkar, Sania Mirza, Ronaldo, Milkha Singh, Messi , Pawan Sehrawat , Lewis Hamilton and so on.

Oh, don't worry being master of that sport isn't necessary. Just play it fluently and most importantly enjoy it

****

<u>Writing a Book...</u>

Everyone says writing a book is a easy job

But when you start to do, you realize that

Noooo

It's not an easy job

Always finding perfect thinking to create a perfect sentence,

Having no mistakes

Perfect grammer and what not

But don't worry we got our editorial
board friends

The one who helps in grammer,
errors and many more

I am as the author very thankful to
them

I hope by my dearest heart that you
all will always support me

Keep in mind, that writing a book is
never easy

****

<u>Mystery of Washing machine</u>

It's arriving today... oh yes its arriving today

I will give you a hintttt

It's a thing which is electronic ....

Many people use it to wash their clothes

While washing they separate the white ones in fear that the other colorful clothes will spread their colors

In the white world

The little ones think they have
someone inside there doing the
laundry.

But who will tell their little heart
that.....

There is no person just the
mechanism

This thing come in two types..

The frontload and the top load

Even though they do the same work

Now you must have understood that

It's a washing machine....

Our old one got tired and stopped
working

So because of its laziness we need
to purchase the new one now

So the doorbells now ringing

Telling that the machine has
arrived...

Let's say bye to the old one

It's arriving today... oh yes its
arriving today

****

<u>Mask</u>

Uhhh. Me and the whole world was
getting frustrated

By wearing this thing on our face
continuously It was so frustrating

But in the end its for our own
safety purpose

It protected us like a mighty soldier

giving its best

It's the mask

I am thankful to you for protecting
me

and the others by the deadly
covid19

The time was of disaster....

People were remembering the old
memories of the good times

Everyone was confused, scared and
waiting for help

Exams were cancelled....

They were now online

The world was on lockdown

Thanks to the doctors, nurses,
social workers who helped us by
breaking their sleep

Even in future forgetting the
experience of covid19 will be hard
for everyone

Anyone... everyone.. me ...you..all this
world has made the history for
surviving this pandemic

Times were hard..times were hard

Uhhh me and the world getting frustrated..

Finally this war has ended

******

My Favorite...Ice Cream

It's finally summer

Time to eat ice cream

But mommy says nooo

Bcoz my exams are not over yet

She is worried that I will fall ill

Finally exams are over

But daddy said no to ice cream

In fear that my throat will get sore

Because I was having an upcoming
music competition

Finally music competition is over

But I don't know if I can have ice
cream

At home I didn't knew that a
surprise was waiting for me

My mom and dad had arranged a ice
cream party

For me!

There was cones, tubs etc

I am so glad that summer is going on

It's finally summer

Time to eat ice cream

****

<u>My Smart Watch</u>

When I was young I decided to do a
collection

But I did not knew about what

First I started to do of coins but
then I understand that this trend is
now old

After that I shifted to stamps

I collected a lot but then I heard
that no one writes letters nowadays

Then again I shifted to colorful
rocks

But the collection finished earlier
than I thought

Now I wondered what collection
should I start?

My mom given me a suggestion of a
collection of smart watches

Then on my birthday I got my first
smart watch

My smart watch collection is still
going on

Now I have watches of amaze fit, mi
bands, noise etc

Year by year the collection is
getting bigger

I love having a collection of smart
watches bcoz it will never end

I get the right for selection

I love my collected smart watches

****

My School

I love my school

Its infrastructure... wow so big and
cool

We got a library full of amazing
books such as

Story books, autobiographies,
biographies, study books as well

The library is very neat and clean

We got a computer lab full of
astonishing computers

We get to use them every
Wednesday and Friday

We got a music roommm

Which has stunning instruments
such as Casio, Tablas, harmonium
and fluteee

It also has a gigantic guitar but we
are not allowed to play it

Only older students are

We also got a sports room where there are kept sports breathtaking supplies

Such as bat and ball, Frisbee, shuttle and rackets, athletics supplies etc

My most favorite is our science lab and tinkering lab

Science lab is all wonderful

We go there for practicals

I am an official member of tinkering lab

We do coding, programming and we also create robots

Ohh it's so much fun

We have nice teacher who helps us

And teaches us wonderfully

We also have a lot of fun activities

Oh I love my school very much

****

www.ingramcontent.com/pod-product-compliance
Lightning Source LLC
Chambersburg PA
CBHW031509150726
47990CB00007B/2940